D1085389

The Aquinas Lecture, 1964

ST. THOMAS
AND
PHILOSOPHY

Under the Auspices of Wisconsin-Alpha
Chapter of the Phi Sigma Tau

by

ANTON C. PEGIS, F.R.S.C., LL.D.

MARQUETTE UNIVERSITY PRESS
MILWAUKEE
1964

76922

BX
1749
T7
P4
1964

Library of Congress Catalog Card Number: 64-17418

To

Etienne Gilson

Teacher and Friend

Prefatory

The Wisconsin-Alpha Chapter of Phi Sigma Tau, the National Honor Society for Philosophy at Marquette University, each year invites a scholar to deliver a lecture in honor of St. Thomas Aquinas, whose feast day is March 7. These lectures are called the Aquinas Lectures, and are customarily given on the second Sunday of March.

In 1964 the Aquinas Lecture "St. Thomas and Philosophy" was delivered on March 8 in the Peter A. Brooks Memorial Union of Marquette University by Dr. Anton C. Pegis, Fellow of the Royal Society of Canada, Professor of Philosophy, Pontifical Institute of Mediaeval Studies, and the University of Toronto.

Professor Pegis was born in Milwaukee on August 24, 1905. He earned his A.B. at Marquette University in 1928 and his M.A. in 1929. In the fall of that year he began his doctoral studies at the Institute of Mediaeval Studies, which had begun that year under the direction of Professor Etienne Gilson and received its pontifical charter ten years later. Two years later Professor Pegis earned his Ph.D. from the University of Toronto and returned to Marquette University as an instructor and then assistant professor. In 1937 he became a member of the graduate faculty of Fordham University. During his last two years at Fordham, Professor Pegis also lectured at the Pontifical Institute of Mediaeval Studies (Toronto). In 1946 he was named President of the Institute, and retained this position until 1954, when he became editor of the Catholic textbook division of Doubleday Publishing Company. He returned to the Institute and teaching in 1961.

In the domain of Christian philosophy, Professor Pegis is a leading American scholar, whose work as editor, lecturer, and teacher has been directed to a better appreciation of the influence of Christian thought on philosophical understanding. In 1946 he was elected president of the American Catholic Philosophical Association. He was chosen to give the third Aquinas Lecture (Marquette University) in 1939, the Gabriel Richard Lecture (St. Louis University) in 1955, the McAuley Lecture (St. Joseph's College, West Hartford) in 1960, and the St. Augustine Lecture (Villanova University) in 1962. His special interest has been the Christian philosophy of man, beginning with his doctoral dissertation on the problem of the human soul. Progressively deeper analysis of this problem has led Dr. Pegis to a new appraisal of what Christian philosophy is or should be, if it were true to the mind of St. Thomas.

His published works include: *The Problem of the Soul in the 13th Century* (Toronto: Institute of Mediaeval Studies, 1934); *St. Thomas and the Greeks* (Milwaukee: Marquette University Press, 1939); *Christian Philosophy and Intellectual Freedom* (Milwaukee: Bruce, 1955); *At the Origins of the Thomistic Notion of Man* (New York: Macmillan, 1963); *The Middle Ages and Philosophy* (Chicago: Regnery, 1963).

He translated and edited the two-volume *Basic Writings of St. Thomas Aquinas* (New York: Random House, 1944) and the one-volume *Introduction to St. Thomas* (New York: Modern Library, 1948). In addition, he edited the English translation of the *Summa Contra Gentiles*, the five-volume *On the Truth of the Catholic Faith* (Garden City: Doubleday and Company, Inc. 1956).

To this list of published works, Phi Sigma Tau is pleased to add: *St. Thomas and Philosophy*.

St. Thomas
and Philosophy

I

When, in the fifth volume of his monumental history of world systems, Pierre Duhem reached St. Thomas Aquinas, what attracted his attention was what appeared to him to be an unresolved situation. Between the philosophy of the philosophers, as expounded by his teacher Albert, and Albert's own Christian philosophy there remained many points of disagreement. Were the arguments of the philosophers conclusive? If so, why did they lead to so many errors about God, creation, man, the soul, and the intellect? Or did philosophy have its own set of "truths," which were "true" because they had been demonstrated while Christianity proposed another set of "truths" known by revelation? In short, as between the philosophers and his own faith, did the Christian live in a sort of no man's land between two worlds whose truths contradicted one another?[1]

The work of St. Thomas was for Duhem the effort of a Christian soul to escape from this perilous situation.

Like his master, he admits that a philosophical truth exists, and that this truth is established by way of reasoning and without borrowing anything from the methods of theology. Like his master, he admits that, in great part, this truth is to be found deposited in the books of those whom Albert called the Peripatetics. He admits likewise that another truth is to be found in the teachings of the Church, from which the theologians take it in order to give it a fuller exposition. Nevertheless he is convinced that these two truths cannot be mu-

1.   Pierre Duhem, *Le système du monde. Histoire des doctrines cosmologiques de Platon à Copernic* (Paris: Librarie scientifique A. Hermann et Fils), V (1917), 468-570. See p. 468.—For a philosophical critique, as rare as it is dated, see Paul Gény, S.J., "La cohérence de la synthèse thomiste," *Xenia Thomistica,* ed. S. Szabó, O.P. (3 vols.; Romae: Typis Polyglottis Vaticanis, 1925). I, 102-25.

tually opposed and that, on the contrary, they must agree with one another in the most harmonious way possible; and all his efforts, it can be said, aim to silence the dissonances that would prevent us from seeing the disagreements between Peripatetic philosophy and Catholic dogma.[2]

In an early work, the little treatise *On Being and Essence,* St. Thomas asked the meaning of essence and existence as metaphysical notions, and how these notions were realized in the different realities that made up the universe. This question brought him face to face with an issue that had agitated all the philosophers and had led to their metaphysical doctrines and their disagreements. At this metaphysical crossroad among the philosophers, St. Thomas the metaphysician was made— and unmade. He met the ideas and principles of Plato and Aristotle, Boethius and Avicenna, *The Book of the Causes,* Iben Gabirol, Averroes and Maimonides; he met them, he did not wholly agree with

2. Duhem, *op. cit.,* p. 469.

them, but neither did he "undertake to set out in an unexplored direction starting from hitherto undiscovered principles." Instead he limited his own initiative to harmonizing the ways followed by his predecessors and to taking from each one of them a part of the way that ought finally to lead to the truth.[3]

This syncretism proved to be the undoing of St. Thomas since, according to Duhem, as a philosopher St. Thomas died of confusion and contradiction; he sought to put together a harmonious teaching drawn, piece by piece, from all his predecessors. He was, by turns, the disciple of his great masters—Avicenna, Augustine, Aristotle—and in his career he moved toward the philosophy of Aristotle as interpreted by Averroes as to his culminating philosophical position. But he held to this position only so long as it did not disagree with Catholic dogma; when forced to do so, he retreated to the views of Avicenna which sometimes allowed him

3. *Ibid.*, p. 470.

a better rapprochement between philosophy and theology. This "retreat from philosophy to philosophy cannot be executed without involving many illogical steps."[4] On the notions of being, matter, individuation, St. Thomas floated back and forth, among contradictory views, without seemingly knowing it. Desiring to reconcile Aristotelianism and Catholicism, which are irreconcilable, St. Thomas adopted all possible retreats from Aristotle in order to keep the ideal of reconciliation alive. The result was philosophical incoherence, achieved in the name of orthodoxy.[5]

Philosophically speaking, then, what is Thomism? In answering this question, Duhem excluded Thomistic theology from his analysis and limited himself to the philosophical field, to the domain that had been marked out by the *Physics* and *Metaphysics* of Aristotle. Moreover, to avoid all possible misunderstanding, Duhem made his question even more restricted

4. *Ibid.,* p. 567.
5. *Ibid.,* p. 568.

and precise: what is philosophical Thomism? And here is the answer:

> If by Thomism is meant a single and coordinated doctrine belonging properly to St. Thomas either through the principles from which it flows or through the order that unites and brings together its several parts, we believe that we can boldly answer the question thus: there is no Thomistic philosophy.[6]

Duhem did not find in St. Thomas a single philosophical proposition of importance that did not belong to some other thinker. Sometimes St. Thomas' source was St. Augustine or the Pseudo-Dionysius; sometimes it was Aristotle or one of his commentators; and sometimes it was Avicenna or Algazel or Moses Maimonides or *The Book of Causes.* From this point of view, the philosophical work of St. Thomas seems like a vast emporium in which we can recognize a whole multitude of distinct pieces taken from all the philosophies of the past. That is why Thomism is not

6. *Ibid.,* p. 569.

a philosophical doctrine but an impulse and an aspiration toward one; it is not a synthesis but the desire of one.[7]

In the presence of all the philosophies of the past St. Thomas was full of respectful admiration. His great predecessors, from Plato to Maimonides, had discovered truth in its totality, and if their systems seemed to disagree, this was because each one of them had only a part of the truth; but if one were to bring them together and combine them judiciously, one would end up by collecting into a whole all that the human reason could discover of the truth. What is more, with the whole of philosophical truth in his hands, one would also not fail to recognize the full accord of this truth with that other part of truth that God has revealed and teaches us through His Church. And so, like a child putting a puzzle together, St. Thomas fitted together the fragments that he had detached from Peripateticism and the various branches of Neoplatonism, convinced

7. *Ibid.*, p. 569.

that these pieces, so different in their shapes and colors, would end up as a harmonious picture, the philosophical image of Catholic dogma.

So great was St. Thomas' desire for a synthesis that, according to Duhem, he even blinded his own judgment and critical sense. It never occurred to him that, however one might separate or even dissociate them from their source, the doctrines of Aristotle, *The Book of Causes*, and Avicenna would never end up by harmonizing with one another; they would remain radically incompatible among themselves, and they would be irreconcilable with the Catholic faith. When, confronted by his juxtaposed fragments of the philosophers, St. Thomas noticed an all too glaring discord, he did not despair of succeeding. He made repeated efforts at a synthesis in order to remove the discord. Sometimes his conviction that the philosophers could be harmonized drove him to force their discord into a synthesis, as a child might force the pieces of a puzzle to fit together. If this result deformed the texts of the philosophers, it was a witness to his unwillingness to believe that a synthesis was impossible or that the philosophers were irreconcilable with one another or with his own Christian faith.[8]

II

The fact that in our day Duhem's case against St. Thomas as a philosopher is some fifty years old does not make it automatically untrue or irrelevant. The further fact that, once formulated, the case may seem to some to be an extraordinary caricature of the attitude and spirit of St. Thomas does not prove that it is groundless. Admittedly, to think that as a philosopher St. Thomas was an incoherent jigsaw puzzle of other people's opinions is a strange idea; to think, moreover, that in the presence of the philosophers and the diversity of their views he died of metaphysical indigestion, is an equally strange notion. The only question is whether, strange or not, Duhem's case against St.

8. *Ibid.*, p. 570.

Thomas does not contain a fruitful point for our examination.

To think of St. Thomas as Duhem had done is to attribute to him two failures. He failed to understand each of the great philosophers before him in any adequate way and therefore, in an effort at a synthesis among them, he produced an incoherent patchwork quilt of discordant philosophical doctrines and opinions. This failure was part and parcel of another one. St. Thomas also failed to formulate a metaphysical doctrine of his own, original and coherent, and one that would have embodied the synthesis that he dreamed of making. But he could not reconcile the philosophers with one another, and he could not achieve the ideal of a harmony between the world of philosophical truth and that of revelation. For, having failed as a philosopher, St. Thomas was also bound to fail as a theologian. How could he defend the unity of truth, however much he proclaimed it, if the philosophers had confused him to the point of incoherence?

Many things have happened in the last fifty years that enable us to set aside part of Duhem's difficulty as historically untenable. A patient reading of St. Thomas makes it quite clear that one of his earliest and most persistent efforts was to establish a fundamental philosophical tradition that he attributed to Aristotle and that he used as a yardstick in interpreting the philosophers. He criticized the various Platonisms that he knew by means of this Aristotelianism, just as he dealt in the same way with such followers of Aristotle as Alexander of Aphrodisias, Avicenna, and especially Averroes. If he could bend his predecessors for the better, he did so and very often he did so silently. He did so especially in the case of Aristotle whom he made into a sort of spokesman for philosophical truth. This was not particularly original or surprising in St. Thomas since some of his contemporaries had gone much farther than he in this regard. In an Aristotelian age, intensely occupied with the writings, the technical language, and the ideas of Aristotle and his followers, the

question was not whether to be occupied
by the intellectual world created by the
Aristotelians, but how best to do it. St.
Thomas' personal originality lay in making
possible a Christian Aristotelianism by
focusing attention on specific Aristotelian
principles and truths, and by using these
truths both to disarm his opponents and
to open the way for his own reading and
use of Aristotle. He could prove, for example, that Averroes was a forced and
unfaithful interpreter of Aristotle's psychology and ethics, just as he could prove
that the doctrine of the eternity of the
world did not mean in Aristotle, as it meant
in Averroes, that the world was uncreated.
Of course, such specific exegetical victories
did not prove that St. Thomas' Aristotelianism was itself the right one; it did show,
however, that his interpretation was an
open possibility to be explored on its
merits.

It is not necessary to argue that St.
Thomas was in full possession of his Aristotelianism, or that he had mastered the history of philosophy, from the beginning of

his career. But if we allow him a scant half dozen years for this purpose, we can say that he was master of his own intellectual household by 1260 at the latest, when, in his middle thirties, he was writing the *Summa Contra Gentiles*. There is nothing incoherent or youthfully immature about *this* Thomas Aquinas. His philosophical attitude was settled, his interpretation of Aristotle was established, and the lines of his own defense of Aristotelianism were clearly set forth. His metaphysical position and its vocabulary were fixed, his use of philosophy in the service of the human communication of sacred doctrine was openly proclaimed, and his individual personality as a theologian was already a classic Christian monument. Here was a man—an extraordinary and single-minded friar, the humble servant of God and of the revealed truth with whose fire the earth had been touched—here was a man, I say, who as a theologian was passionately dedicated to one overall mission in his world: he wanted to show, in relation to the intellectual challenge posed by Aris-

totelianism, that, though Christianity was
a religion and not a philosophy, a divine
truth on earth and not a human discovery,
yet it had a place within itself for the whole
world of philosophical truths. Christianity
could contain every vestige of truth that
the philosophers had ever discovered; and
it could contain all these truths in a synthesis in which whatever truth man could
find in creation was both divine in its
origin and a preamble to the still higher
truth that the same creating God had
chosen to reveal to men.

This description of the work of St.
Thomis in the thirteenth century is almost
a total denial of the views expressed by
Duhem. Of course, description is not
proof, and the question is to know how
a disagreement of such magnitude is possible. Assuming, indeed, that my description is a reasonably faithful picture of
what modern historians are saying about
St. Thomas Aquinas, we are left to wonder
about a rather curious phenomenon. How
could Duhem have been so wrong? How
is it that such an accomplished historian

did not see the synthesis created by St. Thomas? And how is it that he saw so much incoherence and so much philosophical failure? Why did he not find the philosophy of St. Thomas Aquinas, and why did he not see the metaphysical foundation that he had built for it? In part, these questions must remain without an answer; but only in part. Why a historian does not see what others see, or why he sees what they do not, is an unanswerable human problem. In this sense, Duhem's personal vision of St. Thomas must remain unexplained. And yet we can recognize something in that vision that was pointing to a genuine problem, and that, in its very insistence on the philosophical incoherence of St. Thomas, was emphasizing a fact which today we are beginning to appreciate and evaluate in a way that was unknown to Duhem and to Duhem's time.

Duhem had set aside St. Thomas's theology in order to discover St. Thomas' philosophy. In this effort he failed, and he concluded from his failure both that St. Thomas had no personal philosophy and that he was totally unsuccessful in reconciling the philosophers. Now if our present-day ideas are correct, there is something true in Duhem's position. St. Thomas did not have an explicit and articulated personal philosophy, but, contrary to Duhem, we think today that St. Thomas did not have one for a much better reason than the one advanced by Duhem. He had no philosophy, not because he failed in the effort to establish one, but because he never meant to create a philosophical synthesis for whatever purpose. Hence, if it is true that he never meant to be a philosopher, he could not have died of philosophical incoherence in the presence of the philosophers of the past from Plato to Maimonides. And if it be asked: what, then, did St. Thomas aim to be? the answer is: he aimed to be a theologian and, in the presence of the philosophers, he aimed to create a theological synthesis; he therefore set out to formulate philosophical principles in order to use them to the extent that this was necessary for his theology. In such circumstances, if we are to understand and judge the success or failure of St. Thomas in relation to philosophy and in the face of the philosophers, we must evidently first discover what his professional attitude toward philosophy was and how and to what purpose he engaged in it.

Clearly, that Duhem did not find a philosophy in St. Thomas is not at all surprising if it should turn out to be true that there is no autonomously developed philosophy in his personal teaching. Moreover, if St. Thomas Aquinas did not set out to be a philosopher, then it would not be surprising that he did not create a philosophical reconciliation of his predecessors or bring about a synthesis in which they could be seen in a state of philosophical peace with one another. Perhaps Duhem should not have been as surprised as he was at the failure of St. Thomas to reconcile his predecessors since he knew the very reason why they were, in metaphysical terms, irreconcilable. Indeed, does anyone really reconcile his predecessors? If he is fortunate, as well as docile to their very diversities, he may be able to climb through their intuitions to a higher ground and in this way to transcend them; and, having transcended them, he may look back with loyalty and point out how much the road that he has followed is their road and how much they aimed at that common meeting ground where he himself had the good fortune to arrive. But this is not exactly a synthesis, effected by some miraculous fitting together of philosophical pieces that do not belong together; this is a new vision, created by one man, owing to the past everything except its own existence. As concerns St. Thomas himself, the only question is to know what name to give to this new vision. It was not philosophy, and to the extent that it was a vision, new and personal and unique to St. Thomas, it was not a synthesis. What was it? It was a theology, deliberately speaking to the intelligence of man as a theology and using the resources of philosophy in order to communicate to men the teaching and message of revelation.

III

This conclusion is as difficult to accept as it is to understand. The conclusion says that, taking "philosophy" in the sense in which the term has been used since the seventeenth century, there is no "Thomistic philosophy"; in other words, in the sense in which Descartes, Kant, and Hegel can be said to have had their philosophies St. Thomas did not have one because he did not create one. If it is appropriate to suppose that the fundamental and personal teaching of St. Thomas is to be found in his *Commentary* on the *Sentences* of Peter Lombard, in his two *summae,* and in the great *Disputed Questions (On the Power of God, On Truth,* and *On Evil),* then we must characterize the Thomistic teaching as theology in its overall perspective, movement, and purpose. There is no doubt that St. Thomas used a great deal of philosophical matter in these works. There is also no doubt that he knew the distinction between philosophy and theology. The question before us is in what sense, if at all, given that St. Thomas was a theologian, we can attribute a philosophy to him.

Evidently, we ordinarily think that a "Thomistic philosophy" exists. We write books and articles about it, and we give courses on it; it is even a little difficult to know what the philosophy programs of Catholic colleges around the world would be if they did not include titles on various aspects of "the philosophy of St. Thomas." But our question remains. If, in the modern sense of the term, St. Thomas was not a philosopher and did not construct a philosophy, what is it that we are teaching as his philosophy? To apply his own distinction between philosophy and theology to St. Thomas himself would tell us either that he knew the distinction, just as he knew from the philosophers what it meant to be a philosopher, or that, in the name of the distinction itself, he intended to be a theologian and knew what he was doing. The distinction could not invent a Thomistic philosophy if St. Thomas Aquinas did not create one. Moreover, the fundamental reason why Duhem did not find St. Thomas

the philosopher visible in the Thomistic
writings was because he was not there.
We know today that a theologian was
there, using and following philosophical
principles within the world of theology,
but present within philosophy for the
transcendent reasons of Christian doctrine.
Is it possible that, in discovering and
teaching what we call the philosophy of
St. Thomas, we have erected into a philosophy only such philosophical principles
and notions that St. Thomas used in and
for his theology? Is it possible that we are
attributing a philosophy to St. Thomas by
identifying it with what was in him a theologically managed and developed reality?

I have asked these questions as part of
an effort to understand what the "philosophy" of St. Thomas was. In the last fifty
years we have discovered medieval philosophy in general, and the philosophy
of St. Thomas in particular, gradually and
by stages. In part, this process has meant
unlearning some of the prejudices that we
have inherited from the nineteenth cen-

tury. But this is a separate story.[9] In part, too, this same process has meant coming to terms with a notorious historical problem, namely, the relations between ancient philosophy and Christianity and, more specifically, their influence on one another when the ideas of Plato, Aristotle, and Plotinus lived again in a Christian world within the minds of St. Augustine and St. Anselm, St. Albert and St. Thomas, St. Bonaventure and John Duns Scotus. What happened to Greek philosophy when it became Christianized or, at least, came to live in a Christian climate? And what happened to Christianity itself during that same process? To limit ourselves to St. Thomas, how are we to understand the relations between Christianity and Aristotelianism in his case? Even if we acknowledge that he Christianized Aristotle and, in turn, Aristotelianized Christianity, to some extent at least, the question is to know what kind of synthesis was produced

9. See A. C. Pegis, *The Middle Ages and Philosophy* (Chicago: Henry Regnery Company, 1963), pp. 19-65.

in this interchange of influences between Christianity and Aristotelianism. When we speak of St. Thomas' Christian Aristotelianism, what exactly do we mean?

Seen in the perspective of history, the question is far from being unimportant. How did St. Thomas relate Christianity, philosophy, and Aristotelianism to one another in that baffling synthesis that we find in his writings? Early in the sixteenth century there was a controversy on the immortality of the soul, recently called the Pomponazzi affair,[10] whose main burden was to answer this question. If the histori-

10. See E. Gilson, "Autour de Pomponazzi. Problematique de l'immortalité de l'âme en Italie au début du XVIe siècle," *Archives d'histoire doctrinale et littéraire du moyen âge,* XXVIII (1961), 163-279; "L'affaire de l'immortalité de l'âme à Venise au debut du XVIe siècle," in *Umanesimo Europeo e Umanesimo Veneziano* (Firenze: Sansoni Editore, 1963), pp. 31-61. With particular reference to Cajetan see the substantial introduction of M. H. Laurent, O.P., to P. I. Coquelle's edition of the Commentary on the *De Anima: Thomas De Vio Cardinalis Caietanus: Commentaria in De Anima Aristotelis,* (Romae: Apud Institutum "Angelicum," 1938), I, vii-lii.

cal Aristotle had not proved the immortality of the individual human soul, and did not really believe in that soul as an intellectual substance, how was it that St. Thomas proved out of Aristotle that the human soul was both an intellectual substance in its own right and the form of matter at the same time? If such a doctrine was not Aristotelian, on what ground did St. Thomas call it Aristotelian and, what is more critical, how did he derive from Aristotle a conclusion that the philosophy of Aristotle could not support?

The sixteenth-century controversy does not directly concern us here, except for one point. What were the relations between philosophy and Aristotle in St. Thomas' mind? Did he identify philosophy with Aristotle or, what is entirely different, Aristotle with philosophy? The difficulties of both Cajetan and Pomponazzi on the immortality of the soul presuppose that St. Thomas identified philosophy with Aristotle and therefore that his own philosophy was an Aristotelianism that could literally be discovered and verified in the text of Aristotle himself. This would mean that St. Thomas was an Aristotelian on fundamentally Aristotle's ground, not on his own, so that whatever philosophy St. Thomas had was in principle identifiable with the philosophy of the Philosopher. Is this what St. Thomas did? If so, the intellectual misfortunes of Cajetan are there to prove that the Thomistic synthesis was a failure; it was a failure because, in the end, the historical Aristotle could not speak any greater or better truths than his own foundations would permit, and to make him a spokesman of such Christian truths as the immortality of the soul was to expose these same truths to the fate that overtook them in Cajetan and Pomponazzi. Let us agree that if Thomistic philosophy is Aristotelianism, such a fate is inevitable, but let us also recognize that the result is as necessary as its premises. We must therefore repeat our question. Did St. Thomas identify philosophy with Aristotle or Aristotle with philosophy? What are we to understand by his Christian Aristotelian-

ism both as "Christian" and as "Aristotelianism"?

During the period between the two
world wars, or, roughly, from 1920 to 1940,
the historians of St. Thomas Aquinas discovered his philosophy in a most decisive
way. From Del Prado to Gilson, not to
exclude such eminent names as Rousselot,
Roland-Gosselin, Sertillanges, and Forest,
the students of St. Thomas Aquinas discovered his intellectual perspective as a
thinker, his basic metaphysical intuitions,
his creation of new philosophical ideas,
and his transformation of old ideas,
whether Greek, Jewish, or Arabian, as part
of the effort to express new philosophical
realities in the Christian world.[11] Naturally,
what St. Thomas did to, and with, the

11. This point is such a massive reality that it
scarcely needs documenting. But it may be
useful to re-examine the state of the discussion
on the originality of medieval thinkers (including especially St. Thomas Aquinas) in
relation to Aristotelian philosophy as presented
by Gilson in 1932: see *L'ésprit de la philosophie médiévale* (2 vols.; Paris: Librairie
Philosophique J. Vrin, 1932), I, 297-324; II,
279-90.

philosophy of Aristotle occupied the historians in a particular way, but the distinctiveness and the originality of the Thomistic synthesis, including especially its own metaphysical foundations, were the central object of their investigation. As a result of their work, and particularly the work of Gilson, we have come to discover (some would say, to rediscover) what has in recent decades been best known as the Christian philosophy of St. Thomas Aquinas. This name is, in reality, both a historical conquest and a battle cry, or, at least, an embattled standard requiring those who uphold it to explain its authenticity and its legitimacy.

As we look back to some thirty years ago when St. Thomas achieved the popularity that he has not since equalled, two ideas in particular stand out as somehow representing his individual signature as a medieval Christian thinker. One of these ideas was common to his world and is embodied in a classic work of interpretation and synthesis published by Gilson in 1932,

The Spirit of Mediaeval Philosophy.[12] The purpose of this work was to show the creative role of Christian theology in the reception and the transformation of Greek philosophical ideas in the Middle Ages and especially in the thirteenth century. The notion of God as a perfect being, a free and generous creator, a loving providence engaged intimately in His creation; the notion of creation as being a radical beginning in existence, suspended within the world of the divine goodness; the further notion of man himself as a free person, whole and autonomous in his very being and experiencing within his liberty the mystery of his return to God—here are notions that medieval theology was provoked into creating at the moment of meeting Greek philosophy and especially Aristotelianism. None of these notions was Greek in origin, though they contained Greek elements and theologians did ex-

12.　See note 11. The English translation of this work was prepared by A. H. C. Downes (London: Sheed and Ward, 1934; New York: Charles Scribner's Sons, 1934).

press them in the language of Aristotle. Moreover, while native to Christian theology, they were philosophical in their nature as ideas and capable of leading their own existence once they had been created. They formed part of what may properly be designated by the historians as a "Christian philosophy": they were philosophical ideas whose historical origin was religious.

St. Thomas Aquinas shared such a Christian philosophy and he gave it a distinctive form by the character of his own metaphysical ideas and principles. Three interrelated ideas especially marked his attitude as a Christian thinker. The idea that God is the pure act of being, that creation is an absolute origin and dependence in existence and not simply a beginning in time, and that metaphysics has to do with being seen uniquely and exclusively in the light of its existence—these ideas constitute in their togetherness the distinctive trademark of St. Thomas in philosophy. What has been called his existentialism is rooted in these ideas and in his employment of them both to bring Christian thought to a new consciousness of its teaching and to give to Aristotelianism a new foundation and a new life within the world of that teaching. It is this latter point that concerns us in the present discussion.

IV

Between Christian theology and the philosophy of Aristotle St. Thomas interposed a metaphysics of being that was his own creation and that revolutionized the meaning of whatever notions he took from Aristotle. This metaphysics was not developed by St. Thomas in its own right or for its own sake but rather as an intellectual tool enabling him to see and to use ancient philosophy within a perspective that had never been its own. It was St. Thomas who said that the ancients were on the way to the idea of creation but did not quite reach it, though they had the principles by which to do it; it was St. Thomas who more than once saw the principles of Plato and Aristotle as capable of serving conclusions that these philosophers had never held; and it was St. Thomas who, in the name of truths that he held in his own right, judged the distance of others from these truths and located them accordingly. Plato and Aristotle became St. Thomas' predecessors only after he saw and said that they were. Plato's philosophy of essence and Aristotle's philosophy of substance became the predecessors of St. Thomas' philosophy of existence when he himself, having seen being from the standpoint of existence, likewise located essence and substance as partial aspects of being. The metaphysical world within which St. Thomas gave such an honored place to Plato and Aristotle was his own, and if he made Aristotle the technical spokesman of philosophy it was in the name of the metaphysics of such a world and not in the name of the historical metaphysics of Aristotle himself.

Two difficulties, not to say obstacles, have prevented students of St. Thomas from appreciating his originality in the presence of Aristotle. One is the fact that St. Thomas seems to have created his own philosophy, not for its own sake or with any view to building a philosophy, but as a link between Christian theology and Aristotelianism. If we do not always see the philosophical ideas of St. Thomas in their own right, this is because they are usually embedded in their service as an intellectual bridge opening Christianity to philosophy and giving to Aristotelianism an adequate metaphysical foundation within Christian thought. The intellectualism that joins Aristotle to Christianity is St. Thomas' own creation. It is such an effective creation that, most of the time, we tend to see only the result that it has made possible, namely, the Christian Aristotelianism that speaks for philosophy and for philosophical truth in the main areas of human knowledge in which the theologian is particularly interested. Yet this Aristotelian edifice lives as a Thomistic creation, and so long as we recognize it as such there is no particular harm in thinking of it as an "Aristotelianism." The only trouble is that when we think of it as a kind of Aristotelianism, forgetting the contribution of the mind that created it, we are regularly puzzled by it. We are particularly puzzled when we try to duplicate it by adding Christianity and historical Aristotelianism to one another. We then discover, as Cajetan and Pomponazzi discovered, that the result does not add up to the Christian Aristotelianism of St. Thomas himself. And assuredly it does not, since St. Thomas proceeded, not by adding, but by creating. He created a metaphysical doctrine, he installed it within his theology as its instrument, and he then created his own Aristotelianism on the foundation of that doctrine.

There is a second difficulty that has served to obscure the personal contribution of St. Thomas to his own Aristotelianism. Here we are in the presence of a far-reaching and even embarrassing issue. It is embarrassing, is it not, to say to those who are teaching Thomistic philosophy that St. Thomas Aquinas was not a philosopher but a theologian? There are recognizable Thomistic principles and there is a recognizable Thomistic outlook, but

there is no autonomous Thomistic philosophy created by St. Thomas himself. Now
if St. Thomas was a theologian, how can
we learn philosophy from him? Indeed,
can we do so? Can we learn philosophy
from the *Summa Theologiae* and from the
Summa Contra Gentiles? Here we are in
the presence of that baffling Thomistic
synthesis and our problem is to know how
to read it in order not to misread it. If St.
Thomas incorporated his philosophy within his theology and intended it to be a
part of that theology, how do we read it
as he meant it unless we read it as theology? And if we read it as theology, what
are the conditions under which we can
then venture to think of it as philosophy?

Since such questions affect the very
nature of the Thomism that we are teaching as philosophy, we must evidently find
satisfactory answers to them. How do we
know that we can teach philosophy from
theological works, that is to say, from
writings that have a theological perspective, synthesis, and purpose? How do we
know that by this procedure we are not

teaching theology, as our critics often enough accuse us of doing? If we stick to those texts in the *Summa Theologiae* that are philosophical in their matter (for example, texts that have to do with natural theology, psychology, and ethics), by what right do we assume that parts or fragments of a theological whole somehow become philosophy by being separated from that whole? Let us assume that there are philosophical parts in the two *summae*, by which I mean discussions about God, man, and human conduct that are fully investigable by the human reason; but let us also suppose that these discussions are parts of a theology, so that they are at one and the same time philosophical in their matter and theological in their location and presentation: what then? Are they philosophy, on the ground of their matter, or theology, on the ground of their treatment? Is a detached piece of theology— say, the so-called treatise on man in the first part of the *Summa*—philosophy or theology?

And yet, in spite of its matter, what is a detached piece of theology? Is it not a lifeless part of a once living whole, lifeless because torn from the intellectual life and vision that sustained it in the mind of the theologian? Ideas, after all, are not mental furniture, not even ideas on paper; they cannot be shifted around from room to room. Ideas are the life of the mind itself, and they are shaped by the purposes of that mind: ideas, let us repeat, are not mental counters for the mind to play with. Even their meaning as an intellectual discourse depends on the mind that thinks them rather than on their matter. The so-called treatise on man is a theologian's vision of man, created by him at a certain moment in history and answering to the problems of his age as he saw them.[13] Its

13.   The treatise on man (*Summa Theologiae* I, qq. 75-89) is dominated by what St. Thomas has called the *consideratio theologi,* whose effect he has pointed out no less than three times (*Sum. Theol.* I, q. 75, Prol.; q. 78, Prol.; q. 84, Prol.). The effect is noticeable in two ways: (1) the study of man is centered in the soul, not directly in the composite as the doctrine itself requires; (2) the study is primarily

point of focus is strictly theological (the *consideratio theologi*), the point of emphasis is on the soul and not on the composite, and its entire organization reflects throughout the perspective of this religious vision.

interested in the intellect and its main concern is historical, exegetical and prudential rather than doctrinal. In the presence of various Aristotelianisms and Platonisms, St. Thomas wishes, not to expound a theory of the human intellect, but, in the midst of conflicting opinions and controversial issues, to enforce the notion of the intellect as something whole, with a specificity of being and operation that belongs to it according to its place in creation. The first two questions of the treatise deal with what may be called the twin foundation stones of any Christian doctrine of man: the human soul is an incorruptible and immortal substance (q. 75); the human person is, as a composite, a true unitary substance (q. 76). But St. Thomas nowhere explains, except indirectly, the third pillar of his doctrine, namely, the proportion between an intellectual soul and an organic body. A *philosophy* of man, based on the doctrine of St. Thomas as distinguished from his theological perspective, would rest on the immortality of the soul and the unity of the human person as on its metaphysical presuppositions; but it would derive its immediate structure and organization *as a doctrine* from the principle of the proportion between soul and body.

Detached from the *Summa* and its specific purpose, the treatise on man is neither philosophy nor theology. It is, to apply to it the severe but appropriate expression that Maritain has used in another context, a piece of lifeless and sterile theology: *une théologie dégermée.*[14] For if the informing vision of St. Thomas himself makes the treatise on man a theology—I mean, a theologically centered and motivated presentation of philosophical materials—why is not that treatise, when bereft of its guiding vision, no more than a lifeless corpse?

I know the standing answer to this question. Why cannot these same materials, being in themselves philosophical, become informed by a philosophical life in the mind of a living Thomist? Thus informed, why is not the treatise on man a living philosophy? Or am I arguing that Thomism can be only a theology because in St. Thomas himself, its unique creator,

14. J. Maritain, *La philosophie morale. Examin historique et critique des grands systèmes* (Paris: Librairie Gallimard, 1960), p. 8.

it was a theology? If this is my position, then, admittedly, it is a vulnerable one. For I seem to be saying, at one and the same time, that there is a visible philosophy at work in the two *summae* of St. Thomas but that, though we see it there, we cannot study it or consider it as philosophy because in the *summae* it is theology. I thus seem to be offering the present-day philosophical student of St. Thomas two choices: learn theology because St. Thomas' philosophy lives with a theological light, or content yourself with philosophical ideas that are no more than dead fragments of a theology.

I hope and think that these are not inevitable choices, and I certainly have no wish to make them mine. But we are in the presence of a strange phenomenon and a strange experience when we undertake to learn philosophy from a theologian with a view to becoming philosophers and not theologians. Let us admit that a theologically managed philosophy—philosophy used and shaped by the theologian in his world and for his purposes—is not philosophy. In the theologian's perspective philosophy is experiencing a guidance and is subject to an economy that both lie beyond its own power to manage. If we wish to learn philosophy, and even to try to be philosophers, we do not wish to accept a theologically managed philosophy as a substitute since it is theology and not philosophy. On the other hand, a theologically managed philosophy that poses as a philosophy by detaching itself from its theological management is still a theology, but a theology in ruins, much like a palace in which there used to live a king but in which now no one is living. A theology without the presence of its manager is a helpless reality. It cannot explain its organization or its order, its perspective or its direction. Let us recognize a crucial fact, which for some of us may also be a cruel one. A living philosophy cannot be derived by detaching a part of theology from the whole in which it once lived. We cannot derive "Thomistic philosophy" by removing it, part by part, from the living edifice that was St. Thomas' theology. A

Thomistic philosophy constructed in this way is not a philosophy but a dead piece of theology.

The point of this conclusion does not have to do with whether or not St. Thomas had a philosophy; it has rather to do with whether we ourselves can reach that philosophy, given that it was a part of his theology. As a theologian, St. Thomas used philosophy, even his own philosophy; he therefore formulated philosophy in a state of service within theology and its economy. The philosophy that we see in the *summae* is a Christian philosophy in a state of being used by theology. Moreover, it is a philosophy whose specific historical function seems to have been to assimilate the world of Aristotelian philosophy and to do so within the religious world of Christianity. However visible Thomistic "philosophy" may be to the modern historian, therefore, there are at least two senses in which it is not visible because it is enclosed within its service. It is a philosophy living within the mind and purpose of a theologian, serving his theological ministry; it is a philosophy which, on its own ground, is serving the assimilation of Aristotelianism. If we do not identify the philosophy of St. Thomas either with its religious service, which would be to think of it as the theology that in fact it was, or with the Aristotelianism for whose technical world it served as the foundation; and if, having made these refusals, we further refuse to identify the philosophy of St. Thomas the theologian with a detached and therefore fragmented piece of his theology, can we still find his philosophy? Having recognized that philosophy to be invisible by reason of its religious mission as a theological instrument serving the further and historical mission of assimilating the philosophy of Aristotle, can we still see it visibly present in St. Thomas?

The answer to this question must be that we can, but that we must look for it in the form in which it is present in St. Thomas. In other words, we must look for it in a man who was a professional theologian and who spent a great deal of time shaping the ideas of others, and chiefly

those of Aristotle, for use in his vision of
the whole universe from the point of view
of the divine mind.[15] In the presense of the
philosophers, St. Thomas was anxious to
take every bit of truth that they had, however imperfect or embedded in error, and
however much they disagreed with one
another in the way in which they reached
the same conclusion—for example, the conclusion that the universe had a first principle or cause whom Christian theology
knew as God. St. Thomas was aware that
the philosophers disagreed with one another, but he could often see a common
truth at work in their very disagreements.
When the problem before him, as he saw
it, demanded that he engage in the disagreement, he did so, and he then corrected some philosophers in the name of
the principles of others; sometimes he
corrected all of them in the name of the
principles of Aristotle; or sometimes,

15. See the admirable text of the *Expositio
    super Librum Boethii De Trinitate* q. II, a. 2,
    ed. Bruno Decker (Leiden: E. J. Brill, 1955),
    pp. 86-87.

though much more rarely, he corrected
even Aristotle himself in the name of
principles that we can only call Thomistic.
But often the Angelic Doctor stood among
the philosophers as a theologian who lis-
tened to their truths and was more anxious
to gather these truths, and the philosophers
themselves, within the light of his theology
than to detail their disagreements or their
errors. Why should not a theologian,
speaking for divine truth among men,
open as many doors as possible to the
presence of that truth on earth?

St. Thomas was such a theologian. He
had a tactical attitude toward the philosophers that can easily be misunderstood as
a willingness to conciliate them. He was
concerned, above all, to lead the philosophers to the truth and to show them by
their own steps, as long as these were
available, that the truth they were seeking
lay in Christian theology. After reading
him for a number of years, we become
aware of what may be called his management of his own discussion, and by a kind
of instinct we look beneath the surface of

his exposition in order to find the point at issue in his mind. That point belongs to his world, and not necessarily to ours; consequently, unless we are willing to follow him in his purposes and in the context of the discussion he had with his own age, he will escape us in our very reading of him. It is too late for us to disagree with St. Thomas in the purposes that he set himself within the thirteenth century. But, since those purposes are embodied in his writing, it is also too late for us to find therein anything but what is contained in the historical letter of what St. Thomas wrote.

To rediscover St. Thomas' purposes in the concrete, to see him at work in his own world and under his own judgment of how to react to that world, this is our only chance of catching a glimpse of that most elusive of realities, his philosophy. It is easy to invent what that philosophy might have been had he not been a theologian, and some have invented it. It is easy to identify it with the Philosopher he created out of the historical Aristotle, and

many have done this too. What is not easy,
and in the end the only thing worth trying
to do, is, beyond such inventions, to see
the shape and spirit of the philosophy that
St. Thomas the theologian did create. And
once we begin to stand with docility in the
presence of this reality, seeking simply to
see it and to understand it, we realize
that we are confronted by something that
is neither the theology that it served (including the form of that service) nor the
Aristotelian materials that it used to expound the word of God to men. At this
precise moment we are face to face with
the spirit of the personal philosophy of St.
Thomas Aquinas reflected in the mirror of
the theology that both created and nourished it. It is that spirit, seen in the theologian's vision of it, that we must try to
recapture as the distinctive signature of
the philosophy that St. Thomas never
spoke as a philosopher because he chose
to use it in speaking as a theologian.

V

Perhaps the most personal work that St.
Thomas Aquinas wrote as a theologian was

the *Summa Contra Gentiles.* It is personal
because in it he gave expression to a rare
public profession of his vocation as a theologian. It is personal also in another sense.
It contains a distinctive occupation with
philosophy, and especially with Aristotelianism; so much so that historians have
wondered about its purpose, including its
plan and organization. And well they
might wonder. Divided into four books,
and devoted to an exposition of the truth
professed by the Catholic faith, the work
proceeds in a surprising way if it aims
to be a theology. Relegating to the fourth
book the two central truths of Christianity, namely, the Trinity and the Incarnation, it devotes the first three books to
those truths of faith that are investigable
by reason; moreover, it does so in such a
way that some historians at least have
wondered whether the first three books
are not philosophy whereas only the fourth
book is, properly speaking, theology.[16] As

16. For the earlier bibliography on the question
    of the plan and purpose of the *Summa Contra
    Gentiles,* see my introduction to the English

late as 1948, in the sixteenth volume of its
edition of the works of St. Thomas Aquinas, the Leonine Commission committed
itself to this interpretation of the *Summa
Contra Gentiles*.[17] One can sympathize
with such a decision without accepting it.
The first three books of the *Summa Contra
Gentiles* are so full of philosophical principles, analyses, and problems, that it is not
easy to remember that St. Thomas is there
dealing with investigable truths of faith.
The eminent Dominican M.-D. Chenu,
was, without question, on much more solid
ground when in 1950 he reasserted the
idea that the *Summa Contra Gentiles* was
a theological work with a deeply historical
occupation, namely, the effort to meet the

translation of the first book *St. Thomas Aqui-
nas: On the Truth of the Catholic Faith*, Book
One: God (Garden City, N.Y.: Doubleday &
Company, Inc., 1955), pp. 54-55.

On faith as having principally to do with the
Trinity and the Incarnation, see *Sum. Theol.*
II-II, q. 1, a. 6, ad 1; a. 8; *Compendium The-
ologiae* cc. 1-2.

17.   *Sancti Thomae Aquinatis Doctoris Angelici
Opera Omnia . . . . Tomus Decimus Sextus:
Indices* (Romae: apud Sedem Commissionis
Leoninae, 1948), pp. 285-93.

new Aristotelianism confronting the Christian world in general and Christian theology in particular.[18]

Anyone who is willing to accept St. Thomas' word for what he is doing can scarcely disagree with Father Chenu. St. Thomas has said more than once that, in writing the *Summa Contra Gentiles,* he is concerned with the two kinds of truth revealed by God to men. There is the order of truth about God that men can arrive at by rational investigation but which, in the concrete circumstances of human life, it would be enormously difficult for them to reach; there is also the order of truth that men can never come to know but that they need to know if they are to direct themselves properly to the destiny for which in fact God has created them. The existence of God, the doctrine of a free creation, and the notion of a divine providence creatively present in the universe are the outstanding examples of the first

18. M.-D. Chenu, O.P., *Introduction à l'étude de sainte Thomas d'Aquin* (Paris: Librairie Philosophique J. Vrin, 1950), pp. 247-54.

order of truths; the doctrines of the Trinity and the Incarnation are the chief examples of the second order. It was St. Thomas' aim to show, by demonstration in relation to the first order of truths and by authority in relation to the second, not only the validity of the claims of Christianity as a religion but also the internal unity of the Christian world of truth; and he undertook to show this unity by setting forth the harmony between the truths about God reachable by demonstration and the truths knowable to man only by revelation.[19]

And yet the very form of the *Summa Contra Gentiles* offers a serious puzzle to the modern historian. Given that the work is a theology, it yet postpones the central truths of Christianity to the fourth and last book. On the other hand, the later *Summa Theologiae* was to unfold the whole history of man and the universe by beginning with the Trinity and ending with the Incarnation and its consequences.

19. See especially *Summa Contra Gentiles* (=*S.C.G.*), I, c. 7.

If both *summae* are theologies, how is it that they are organized so differently? How is it that as a theology the *Summa Contra Gentiles* spends so much of its time on those Christian truths that fall under revelation but are demonstrable? These are unavoidable questions, requiring the student of St. Thomas to distinguish between the specific human purposes of the two *summae* and to define with some precision the aim that governs the *Summa Contra Gentiles* as a theology.

There may be many ways of formulating the human purpose of the *Summa Contra Gentiles,* depending on the particular teaching of the work that happens to interest the student. But St. Thomas' very willingness to devote three out of its four books to those doctrines of the Christian faith that are also demonstrable and can fall within the range of philosophy is noteworthy to the point of being the outstanding phenomenon in the whole work as a theology.[20] What was St. Thomas' human

20. In spite of this fact, it has recently been proposed that the S.C.G. has no historical

purpose? What objective did he have in mind? As a working hypothesis I shall propose here the view that the *Summa Contra Gentiles* was written at the very same crossroad where Duhem had already found St. Thomas, but it was written by a man who wished to stand among the philosophers as a theologian and who had something both to learn and to teach in their presence.

From Aristotle especially St. Thomas wished to learn the nature and technical order of philosophy. What did a philosophical examination of the universe and of man consist in, and what destiny did Aristotle hold up for men in the name of their intelligence and therefore in that of philosophy itself? What did Aristotle have to say about the nature of God and His

purpose and no historical roots in its age. See the introduction of R. A. Gauthier, O.P., to the first volume of the now complete Latin-French edition of the *S.C.G.*: *Saint Thomas d'Aquin: Contra Gentiles, Livre Premier*, trans. R. Bernier and M. Corvez, Intro. R. A. Gauthier (Paris: P. Lethielleux, 1961), pp. 87-123.

relations to the universe, including His relations to man? These things St. Thomas wanted to learn in order to enter into the same truths as a theologian and to show wherein, after the errors and the misdirections of the philosophers had been removed, the aim of philosophy was contained and verified within the theology that he himself professed. Believing in the unity of truth, indeed, in the divine origin of the very principles with which the human intellect was endowed, St. Thomas went so far as to hold that whatever was opposed to these principles was contrary to the divine wisdom.[21] How, then, could the Christian faith contradict or oppose

21. "Item. Illud idem quod inducitur in animam discipuli a docente, doctoris scientia continet: nisi doceat ficte, quod de Deo nefas est dicere. Principiorum autem naturaliter notorum cognitio nobis divinitus est indita: cum ipse Deus sit nostrae auctor naturae. Haec ergo principia etiam divina sapientia continet. Quicquid igitur principiis huiusmodi contrarium est, divinae sapientiae contrariatur. Non igitur a Deo esse potest. Ea igitur quae ex revelatione divina per fidem tenentur, non possunt naturali cognitioni esse contraria." (S.C.G. I, c. 7, #2.)

the truths of Aristotle or fear his demonstrations?

The notion that seems to have united St. Thomas' effort as a theologian into a single overall objective, dominating not only his doctrinal synthesis but also his Christian apologetic before the bar of human intelligence, was the nature and meaning of the divine transcendence—the transcendence of that God Whom the philosophers had made remote in order to free Him from the vicissitudes of the universe, but Whom St. Thomas wished to make, in the name of His very transcendence, an intimately present God, a God Who was involved in His creatures and Who went before them in all that they were and did. The doctrine of a creative divine providence, infinitely transcendent and yet immanent in the world, was the frontier to which St. Thomas wished to lead the philosophers and philosophy itself. Indeed, it was more than a frontier, being a new world for philosophy and a new awakening for human intelligence. How did a man philosophize in a world that was not only the orderly universe known to the great ancient philosophers, but also the voice of a creating God addressing itself to man as a person and evoking from him the awareness that he was living in the world as in the presence of a personal creator and that he could live there, in such a mysterious presence, only by engaging and committing himself as a person?

On the whole, we have not been sufficiently aware of the personalism of St. Thomas' thought and particularly of the personalism to which he opened the philosophy of Aristotle. We have tended to look at the teaching of the *Summa Contra Gentiles* more or less impersonally and to take for granted the Christian world within which St. Thomas made Aristotle into the Philosopher. As a result, we have tended not to see the intellectual revolution that is going on before our eyes. We are not surprised that St. Thomas makes the Prime Mover of Aristotle into the God of Christianity, the perfect Being Who is also a free creator and a loving providence;

nor are we surprised that St. Thomas has
changed the Aristotelian ethics into an
ethics of this life, imperfect and temporal
in its beatitude, but looking beyond the
present to the perfect beatitude of eternal
life. And yet, these changes are more than
mere corrections or even transformations of
Aristotelian philosophical notions, and St.
Thomas did more than improve Aristotelian doctrine in the process of making it
Christian. The most radical part of his
accomplishment, and one that we scarcely
see, is that he created the human intellectual climate within which Aristotle
could be transformed into the Philosopher.

For the first time in its history Aristotelianism became, in the world of St.
Thomas, a new reality; it became a personalist philosophy, a philosophy that, in
its intellectual impulse and movement, was
open to the presence of a transcendent
creator within man's intelligence. St.
Thomas transformed Aristotelianism in
this radical way because as a theologian
he could receive the historical Aristotle
into Christianity only through the medi-

ation of such a step. Otherwise, he could not teach or enforce one of the dearest aims of his theology, namely, to show to the philosophers that a properly conducted philosophy would end, even when it did not know it, within the world of the divine revelation. When, in the mind of St. Thomas, Aristotelianism began to serve the intellectual life of man on his way to God, seeking his perfect good in God and only in God, it was speaking in the name of a new *human* reality, invested with all the personal awareness of an intellectual creature living in the world of time and history and seeking to locate itself in the presence of God. To enable Aristotelianism to participate as a philosophy in such an outcome, St. Thomas had to create its informing spirit and purpose and he had to recreate Aristotelianism in the image of that spirit and that purpose.

It is not difficult to see, in doctrinal terms, the transformation accomplished by St. Thomas in the fundamental areas of Aristotelian teaching—in metaphysics and physics, and in psychology and ethics.

Where the Aristotelian highest science had been a science of the first or highest substances, in St. Thomas it became the science of all being seen in terms of existence.[22] Where the Aristotelian world of motion had been an eternal order of nature ruled by an intelligence that was its unknowing final cause, it became with St. Thomas a world created and governed by an intelligence that was as free as it was intimately involved in its creatures.[23] Where, in the Aristotelian conception of man, animal life and intelligence had never been brought together within a unitary conception of human life, man became successfully unified as a philosophical reality when St. Thomas set out to

22. See E. Gilson, *Being and Some Philosophers* (2nd ed.: Toronto: Pontifical Institute of Mediaeval Studies, 1952), pp. 41-73, 154-89. On Aristotle, see also the conclusions of J. Owens, *The Doctrine of Being in the Aristotelian Metaphysics* (2nd ed.; Toronto: Pontifical Institute of Mediaeval Studies, 1963), pp. 455-73.
23. See *S.C.G.* II, cc. 6-22; to be compared with *S.C.G.* I, cc. 13-22, for the basis of the doctrine, and with *S.C.G.* III, cc. 1, 17-21, 37-40, 48-53, 64-70, for its consequences.

show, not how an animal can be intelligent, but how a certain type of intelligence was endowed with sensibility and needed to be incarnated in matter.[24]

When we turn to the *Nicomachean Ethics,* in which Aristotle outlines the nature and conditions of human happiness, it is much easier to know what St. Thomas did with his teaching than what Aristotle had really meant by it. Did Aristotle really believe that the final destiny of man lay in the present life and that man achieved his share in immortality here and now? But how could he think, as he did,[25] that beatitude was man's perfect good and still believe that man could reach it in the present life? And why speak at all of man's perfect good unless there was some prospect of reaching it? And yet, if man was not endowed with a personal intellectual soul that was incorruptible and capable of surviving the body, what other life

24. See A. C. Pegis, *At the Origins of the Thomistic Notion of Man* (New York: The Macmillan Company, 1963).
25. Aristotle, *Nicomachean Ethics* I, 7. 1097a7.

could man look forward to? In the presence of these Aristotelian issues, St. Thomas made the *Ethics* into a treatise dealing with the happiness of man in this life. He did so as a theologian, recognizing as an interpreter of Aristotle that he was by-passing some embattled problems in order to make the *Ethics* a usable work in the Christian world.[26]

Between the philosophy of Aristotle as so transformed and Christian theology there intervened what I can only call the human reality in whose image the transformation was made. That St. Thomas managed the text of Aristotle in this process can scarcely be contested; that the management was inspired by the deepest religious motives is likewise beyond dispute. But perhaps St. Thomas' religious motives required him to go much further than freeing Aristotle from his errors and shortcomings. The unity of truth was at stake, and while a corrected Aristotle may

26.   I have tried to establish this point elsewhere ("St. Thomas and the Nicomachean Ethics," *Mediaeval Studies,* XXV [1963], 10-17).

not have spoken any errors, he could not have spoken the truth as St. Thomas understood it. He spoke that truth only because St. Thomas created it and directed Aristotelian philosophy to speak it. What St. Thomas transformed Aristotle *into* contains both the historical Aristotle and the vision of intelligence and philosophy that is St. Thomas' own. That vision is rooted in the doctrine of creation, of man seen as an intellectual creature living under the providence of a creating God, of his life conceived as a way to this God, and of philosophy itself as reflecting the intellectual record of man's personal journey to Him. If the intervening human reality created by St. Thomas, being a means to a religious purpose, is not always visible in its own right, still, for those who will look for it, it is visible in its substance and its results; it is visible as an intellectual bridge created by a theologian in the only way that was worthy of both theology and philosophy, as the ideal of a human reality that could be received by faith and that could, in turn, receive Aristotle.

VI

At this date it does not seem necessary to argue that the idea of creation played a decisive role in these and other transformations of the philosophy of Aristotle. But there are two aspects of the work of St. Thomas, both decisive for philosophy, that stand out just as soon as we recognize that God is creatively present in the universe as the author of its existence, its motion, and its finality. The universe is directed by a personal God to Whom man is related as a person in his very creaturehood. If this is an obvious Christian truth, let us also note with St. Thomas a not-so-obvious consequence, namely, the divine initiative within creation. But for that initiative, things would not be, they would not act, they would not tend to their end; with that initiative, things are in a state of return to their end—indeed, they are being returned by their author. This is what it means for them to be: to be being returned to their end by their creator.[27]

27.   S.C.G. III, cc. 1 and 64.

There is more. By His presence in the universe as creator, God gives to the world a historical character in its very existence unknown to Aristotelianism. A created world is a historical one in its being, since for it to be is to be on the way to its end. As a creature, the world exists within the government of the divine providence, its motion and order constitute a long journey to its destiny and man is a part of that historical journey, a part and even its peak.[28] Here begins the personalism of the Thomistic conception of man and of philosophy. Born within a created universe, and under the impulse of a creating and initiating divine providence, man is face to face with a historical vision of himself, and especially of his intelligence and his liberty, that Aristotle had never known. To live according to what was best in him, namely, his intelligence, was for the Aristotelian man a noble destiny, and however much it was a more-than-human goal, it was a life in which he could share. But,

28. *S.C.G.* III, c. 22.

in the end, while the life of intelligence
somehow introduced man into the world
of divinity, it remained a self-enclosed
destiny: man escaped from his concrete
humanity to his intelligence and there, in
the life of contemplation, he experienced
divinity. This is already a high ideal, but
it is not that of St. Thomas Aquinas; or,
rather, St. Thomas saw this ideal as a step
to another and infinitely higher one. As a
creature, human intelligence lives not only
in the company of divinity but also in its
transcendent presence. How can an intellectual creature not awake as a person to
this creative presence of God within his
intelligence and his will? How can his
intellectual life, including the love that
overflows from it, not become a personal
dialogue with his hidden but present creator? And how, in this dialogue, can man
not see himself as a respondent in a personal encounter rather than merely as an
observer of the universe? How can he not
recognize himself as a person whose af-
firmations and negations, whose commit-
ments and engagements by means of those

absolute words *yes* and *no*, take precedence
in him over the rationality of his gaze?
What, then, is an intellectual creature but
a person in a state of response to his creator, and what is the life of such a creature
except the long history of the growth of
that response?

There is still more. For such an approach
to man, which can be seen unfolding with
dramatic intensity in the third book of
the *Summa Contra Gentiles,* transforms
both the conditions of man's pursuit of
beatitude and the very philosophy in
which, as a man, he expresses that pursuit.
True enough, St. Thomas presents the
problem of human beatitude as a theology
of human destiny. We are everywhere
aware that man's pursuit of beatitude not
only began in God's pursuit of man but
is likewise anticipated, every step of the
way, by this ever-present, initiating, and
persistent God. How much God is doing
for man in order that man may seek and
find beatitude! From this point of view,
the central teaching of the *Summa Contra
Gentiles* is that God is beatitude and that

He has given to man a nature that only
He can satisfy. Related to His intellectual
creature as a creator and a sustaining providence, God precedes all of man's steps
to Him in order to make them possible;
and, in a supreme and unfathomable decision, God has related Himself to man as
Savior, crossing from infinity to the world
of time that man might not despair in his
search for beatitude and lose his way. The
Incarnation is therefore the culminating
moment of St. Thomas' argument in the
presence of philosophy. The Incarnation
raises the intellectual creature to a historical destiny that it could not otherwise
know or reach, but it also opens the vision
of the philosophers—and especially the
Aristotelians, Christian and non-Christian
alike—toward the direction in which the
mystery of human beatitude lies. The
philosophers could not know that God in
fact would give man beatitude and that
the Incarnation was to be the channel of
this gift. But, in the name of man's intellectual nature, they could come to know
with certainty that man can have only God

as his end and he can live within this supreme mystery of human existence in the confidence that God would answer appropriately the questions He had Himself raised in creating the intellectual nature of man.[29]

Within this theological vision of man and his destiny it is possible to see the remarkable change effected by St. Thomas Aquinas within Aristotelianism as a philosophy. Having made it into a philosophy that could speak for man the creature in the presence of his creator, he gave to its intellectual movement the historical shape and direction of a personal reality that was a spiritual journey, a questioning search

29. On beatitude and the Incarnation, see *S.C.G.* IV, 54. The interpretation of *S.C.G.* III adopted here departs from the well-known views of Cajetan, recently reasserted by R. A. Gauthier, *loc. cit.*, pp. 103-20; my reason is the one that enabled Bañes finally to disagree with Cajetan. Within a highly adjusted discussion Bañes correctly maintains that, according to St. Thomas, the desire of the intellect for beatitude is the desire to see God. See D. Bañes, *Scholastica Commentaria in Primam Partem* (Madrid—Valencia: 1934), I, p. 1, q. 12, a. 1, ad 5 (p. 251, col 2).

for location within the world of the divine
providence rather than merely an objective
exposition of abstract notions, a search
that would give to the endlessness of time
a human image and therefore a human
ending within time itself. Man cannot give
himself beatitude? No, being a creature,
he cannot. But, yet, he can give himself
the idea of a perfect good and he can know
that such a good contains his beatitude.
Aristotle knew as much, as St. Thomas was
aware,[30] so that the Christian problem of
the latter was how to incorporate the philosophical notion of a perfect good within
the supernatural view of man's present
life as a *via* to the *patria* of eternal beatitude. Clearly, Aristotle's perfect good
could not be identified with either of the
terms of the Christian conception of beatitude. It was not eternal life, but neither
was it the beatitude of the Christian way-
farer. It was, more than anything else, a

30.   See St. Thomas, *In Decem Libros Ethicorum
      Aristotelis ad Nicomachum Expositio,* ed. R.
      M. Spiazzi (Turin-Rome: Marietti, 1949), Lib.
      1, lect. 9, nos. 106, 107, 111, 129.

human reality, man's own vision of beatitude, the perfect good of his intellectual nature; as such, it was not an end for man to seek. He could live in it as in the constant dream of his nature; he could seek to live more and more in its mystery, but he could not seek it. For he could not reach it, and he knew this, and yet he also knew it to be the end of his nature. How, then, did St. Thomas visualize man's relation to his perfect good? What could he do if he knew that it was his good and that he could not reach it?

What we are looking for, in asking these questions, is the Thomistic conception of the end of man and of the end of philosophy seen from the side of man himself. Toward an end that he knows and cannot reach, toward a beatitude that he knows and cannot give to himself, what can man do that will give to his life an ending, but an ending that neither exceeds man's power nor surrenders his vision of the good of his nature? To ask these questions is to ask what, if anything, philosophy has to say about the end of man; and since,

whatever this be, it is also the goal at
which philosophy itself is aiming, we are
here asking one and the same question.
To this question St. Thomas has given, as
I believe, an answer that is as permanently
true in its humanity as it is absolutely new
within Aristotelianism.

The first part of the answer consists in
recognizing an extraordinary fact about
philosophy: it is, as such, an endless enter-
prise. Insisting with Aristotle that man's
ultimate felicity or beatitude is to be found
only in the contemplation of divine things,
to which the last part of philosophy is devoted, St. Thomas asks in what knowledge
of God this contemplation consists. It does
not consist in the ordinary and confused
knowledge of God that men have almost
by nature, nor in the demonstrative knowledge that some men (including philosophers) have of the universe and God, nor
still in the firm but obscure knowledge that
the Christian believer has of God.[31] But
consider what this means. To eliminate

31. S.C.G. III, cc. 37-40.

these sources of human knowledge in our search for beatitude is to do nothing less than to eliminate, in principle, all the possible candidates of man's present life to the title. We can certainly agree that the famous man in the street can have many ill-defined ideas about God, just as we can agree that the believer is not in possession of his beatitude as long as he is walking by faith toward it. But what about the philosopher? Where does he stand in relation to the contemplation of God in which beatitude somehow consists?

The philosopher can prove the existence of God and on this basis he can go on to study the divine nature. But the philosophical knowledge of God, as St. Thomas sees it, does not contain man's ultimate felicity for three decisive reasons. Whatever its value, it is not common to all men, in fact, only a few men are able to have a philosophical knowledge of God, whereas felicity is a good open to all men.[32] Worse still, a philosophical knowledge of

32. S.C.G. III, c. 39, #2.

God, proceeding by demonstration from
a knowledge of the things that make up
this universe, is soon face to face with a
remarkable phenomenon. Though it can
know that God exists, it cannot know what
He is; indeed, this is so true that the total
unknowability of God's nature to man is
the highest result that philosophy can
reach; so that, having proved the existence
of God, the great effort of philosophy is to
reach God in His eminence and transcendence beyond creation—to reach Him by
unsaying progressively all the things in the
universe that the human mind can know
and know also that they are not God. In
a remarkable sentence St. Thomas has
written: *"Hoc ipsum est Deum cognoscere,
quod nos scimus nos ignorare de Deo quid
sit*: to know God consists in this, that we
know we do not know what God is."[33]
Clearly, human beatitude cannot consist in

33. *In Librum Beati Dionysii De Divinis
    Nominibus*, ed. C. Pera (Turin-Rome: Mari-
    etti, 1950), Cap. VII, lect. 4, #731. Cf. *S.C.G.*
    III, 49, #9: ". . . quid vero sit (scil. Deus)
    penitus manet ignotum." See especially, for
    the doctrine as a whole, *In Boeth. De Trin.*

this exalted but still dark night of the human intellect. Finally, the philosophical knowledge of God, which ends in this unknowing as in its peak, suffers in its ordinary life from all the ills of the human intellect. Ignorance, error, uncertainty, inquiry that is unending and piecemeal, never final and therefore without repose, accompanied by the anguish and suffering of man in this intellectual sea without a port on its horizon—these are man's ordinary companions in the philosophical life; so that, whatever be the consolations that invite the philosopher to live—and even to want to live—among such risks, at least we can be sure that the desire that drives him as a philosopher lies beyond both his grasp and his ken.[34]

St. Thomas is not exactly alone in thinking in this way. But it is possible that we may take this otherwise common attitude to be pointing to a conclusion that St. Thomas does not intend. That philosophy

q. I, a. 2 (ed. cit., pp. 64-67); q. VI, a. 3 (pp. 220-23).
34. S.C.G. III, c. 39, ##1, 3, 4, 5, 6, 7; c. 48, ##3, 4, 5, 6, 8, 9.

is a fallible human work does not mean to him that it has been superseded by the Christian revelation; that it is an endless occupation does not mean to him that it has no human goal or outcome; hence, the proposition that God is an infinitely better source of truth does not mean to him that man must abandon his own inquiry in listening to God's invitation to beatitude or that the philosophical effort to see man's own vision of his destiny through to the end has been rendered historically obsolete by the divine message. How could this be true for St. Thomas Aquinas? After defending in the most absolute way possible the unity of truth and the incorporation of the principles of human intelligence within his theology, how could he abandon the human search for beatitude in midstream? And how could he do it in the name of God's offer of eternal life? If the Christian revelation is in the world not as a rival to any human philosophy but as a transcendent invitation to the truth, how can this invitation not open and even urge philosophy to seek to understand and to achieve itself according to the exigencies of its nature? What is that achievement?

After going over all the possibilities of this life in seeking man's beatitude, St. Thomas has evidently reached an ultimate moment in his inquiry. Where, then, does beatitude lie? There are three things that we know at this critical moment that enable us to take another step. Man's desire of an ultimate beatitude is nothing less than the desire of the perfect good and nothing short of it. Man's desire is fulfillable because he has the intellectual capacity for it, though not the power to reach it.[35] Last and far from least, the human soul is immortal. Surviving the death of the body, it can enable man to think that, in an afterlife about which he otherwise knows nothing at all, his desire for beatitude can be fulfilled. These three notions are all demonstrable truths and, being demonstrable, they raise a question. Under such conditions, how does philosophy locate man in the presence of beatitude? Particularly, how does that philosophy do it

35. *S.C.G.* III, c. 54.

which has served as the human instrument
within St. Thomas' theology?

To this question there is a deeply personalist Thomistic answer; indeed, it is
doubly so, involving man the person in
the presence of a personal God. How is it
that God gave to the animals all the necessary equipment of their nature, so that
they might live, protect themselves and
seek their good, and left man by compari-
son in a state of helplessness? St. Thomas'
answer is simple enough. In the place of
natural armor and equipment, God gave
man reason and hands by which he might
provide for himself; he also gave man a
free choice by which he might be turned to
his beatitude. To achieve beatitude does
not lie within his power except in one way:
he can turn to God as to a friend on the
strength of a principle known to Aristotle
himself, namely, that what we can do
through our friends in a way we can do
through ourselves.[36] What does this mean if

36. *Sum. Theol.* I-II, q. 5, a. 5, ad 1. On *liberum
arbitrium* and grace, see *S.C.G.* III, c. 159;
also *Sum. Theol.* II-II, q. 2, a. 7, ad. 3.

not that man can live in confidence within
the world of the divine providence, he can
respond to it by the free commitment of his
liberty, and he can bring all the risks of human existence to a supreme and personal
test of himself and of his universe, indeed,
of himself in his universe? This is the decision to follow his intelligence and his love
into the mystery of the divine providence
and there to live as one returning the divine friendship. What is more personal
than such a decision or the long road leading to it? What is more personalist than a
philosophy dedicated to teaching man that
his end, the end he can share in by the
use of his reason, his hands, and his liberty,
is to risk himself as a person in the presence
of God and thus to make the world of time
a transcendent encounter with that presence? Let us not forget to add that St.
Thomas gave to philosophy such a personalist spirit as a theologian and in order to
achieve the personalizing of Aristotelianism. The result was a Christian intellectualism in which philosophy had only to
follow the personal steps of man the intel-

lectual creature in order to meet the descending steps of his creator.

VII

Can we learn philosophy from a theologian? This is a question that must be asked at least by those who in our day wish to be philosophers and to claim for themselves some legitimate use of the adjective "Thomistic" but who, at the same time, recognize that St. Thomas himself was a theologian and created a theological synthesis. Duhem did not find any personal philosophy in St. Thomas Aquinas because, after he had set aside the Thomistic theology in which philosophy lived as an instrument, there was no philosophy that he could find. On the other hand, those who have identified Thomistic philosophy with Aristotelianism but without recognizing how much St. Thomas contributed to the philosophical re-creation of the historical Aristotle, have been puzzled to know how St. Thomas could have achieved results in philosophy that Aristotle never did. In point of fact, he did,

but not for Aristotelian reasons; he did so
by identifying Aristotelianism with the
spirit and the purpose of its re-creation,
and by establishing it on the principles that
made this possible. In short, St. Thomas
identified Aristotle with philosophy as he
himself shaped it; he did not identify philosophy with Aristotle. As a result, we
shall never understand the Thomistic synthesis unless we make some effort to see
the personal philosophical contributions of
St. Thomas to Aristotle.

Serving as the human instrument and
vehicle of a theology, itself devoted to
incorporating Aristotelian intellectualism
within Christianity, the philosophy of St.
Thomas is admittedly not a very visible
reality. Yet it becomes visible when we
look for it as it was within the Thomistic
synthesis and if we make an effort to accept it on its own terms. As such, it was
not a philosophy, but the intellectual body
of a theology: it was not man speaking
with his intelligence about God and the
universe, it was the Christian revelation
incarnating itself in human intelligence in

order to speak divine truths among men.
This synthesis is what we call a scho-
lastic theology, which cannot exist without
the technical employment of philosophical
principles and procedures but within
which, nevertheless, human intelligence is
living a life and following a light infinitely
beyond its own. The intellectual world of
St. Thomas was a theological world of this
kind, Christian in its intellectualism and
genuinely intellectual in the form and
shape that it gave to the teaching of revelation. St. Thomas thought that only this
intellectualism was the true Christian
answer to the philosophical intellectualism
of Aristotle—true because the problem at
stake was to show that intellectualism had
a permanent place within Christianity and
to prove to the philosophers that they had
only to be fully and unreservedly faithful
to the human intellect in order to discover
even as philosophers that they were already living within transcendent mysteries
that formed part of Christian teaching.

So understood, the theology of St.
Thomas Aquinas contains within itself

both a lasting Christian monument and a specific historical occupation to which it was dedicated; moreover, our problem today is to remain faithful to his intellectualism by recognizing the concrete outlines of his world. We can do so by seeing that world both as Christian and according to the cultural framework of the thirteenth century, by recognizing his philosophy to be such as it was in his world and not such as it needs to be in our own, and especially by not violently disengaging the principles and the spirit of that philosophy from the theological conditions under which St. Thomas chose to be engaged in philosophy. Perhaps, as we look in the writings of St. Thomas for the shape and character of his philosophy, the most difficult thing for us to remember is that in a world still ruled by the light of revelation, in which human culture is nourished by faith seeking understanding, there need be no question of distinguishing between philosophy as such and its ministerial use within theology. St. Thomas so used philosophy, and he never experienced any need to think of philoso-

phy as a philosopher, though he knew that
Aristotle, Avicenna, and Averroes were
philosophers; nor did he think it unnatural
that, in using philosophy within his theology and therefore beyond its depth, he
was doing any violence to it. If he knew
that philosophy was grounded in the light
of reason, he also knew that reason and
nature were fulfilled in the world of revelation and grace to which they were but a
preamble. How could philosophy suffer in
the world that contained its destiny, even
as it contained the promise of man's destiny? Being more than a philosopher, St.
Thomas gave to his philosophy the freedom of his own theology.

And this is still our problem today. We
are living in a divided world and a divided
Christianity. We are likewise living in an
age of unprecedented intellectual discovery, creation, and power when Christianity, far from being prepared to do what
it did in the thirteenth century, namely, to
receive and assimilate the high intellectualism of antiquity, must re-enter and rediscover the world of modern knowledge

before it can dream again of a Christian intellectualism such as St. Thomas Aquinas and his fellow theologians formulated in their day. It may be a question to know whether thirteenth-century Christianity needed philosophers, but there can be no question that the Christianity of our day does. That is why, in looking to St. Thomas Aquinas for light in this need, we are face to face both with what joins us to him and also with what separates our age from his.

Since the beginning of the nineteenth century we have had many Thomisms in the modern world, but perhaps in our day we have the opportunity not only to profit from their experiences but also to undertake a new reading of St. Thomas Aquinas and a new assessment of our own responsibility in seeking to be philosophical disciples of his teaching. Some one hundred years ago Thomism was reintroduced to the world as a pure philosophy. In the present century, and chiefly between the two great wars, it was discovered to be a Christian philosophy owing many of its ideas to theology, so that as a philosophy it could not be separated from the religious soil in which it grew. The name of Etienne Gilson is inseparably connected with this view. The name of the same eminent historian is connected with the further view held by many today that the philosophy of St. Thomas was not only Christian in its character and spirit but also theological in its mode of expression and development: it was, in fact, the minister and servant of sacred teaching, forming as such an integral part of the theological whole to which it belonged. If this is true, then our question remains. How do we learn philosophy from a theology?

The negative part of the answer to this question is the easier to formulate. If, as we have already said, the Thomistic synthesis was a theological one; if, moreover, that synthesis contained philosophical ideas and principles in a state of ministry to theology, philosophical in their matter and theological in their presentation; if, finally, that synthesis contained the whole world of Aristotelian philosophy as re-created by St. Thomas, then we must say that, if Thomistic philosophy exists, it is not philosophy as employed by theology, it is not the philosophy so employed but detached from its employment, nor is it the historical Aristotelianism that regularly served as St. Thomas' technical philosophical tool. What is Thomistic philosophy after these refusals?

Here each student of St. Thomas must speak for himself. For my own part, I would identify the philosophy of St. Thomas himself with that personalist intellectualism that serves as the human reality employed by the author of the *Summa Contra Gentiles.* It is a philosophy spoken in theology by a theologian; it exists there in its principles, in its overall intellectual framework, and in its personalist direction and spirit. But it does not exist in its own right, and under its own management, as a philosophy. The modern student can see the principles that enabled St. Thomas to transform Aristotle, but he cannot find the philosophy that St. Thomas would have built had he chosen to be a philosopher. The modern student can see that the idea of creation not only transforms Aristotle into the instrument of an existential metaphysics, it also introduces his philosophy into a historical world ruled by a creative providence penetrating man himself to the depths of his personal existence and awareness. So understood, the philosophy of St. Thomas Aquinas aims in its very substance to direct man's vision to his encounter with a transcendent God within the universe; it aims, by the very metaphysical urgency of that encounter, to locate the human person in the known presence of an unknown God. This is the philosophy of St. Thomas in its principles, in its aim, and, above all, in the personalist spirit of its intellectualism. Our own problem is that this philosophy exists in its author for a higher than human purpose. Can we, in the conditions of our own day, give to this same philosophy a human purpose and a human existence without violating the theological dedication that St. Thomas himself wrote into it in creating it?

I would like to think that the Thomists of the future will undertake to give to the personalist philosophy of St. Thomas an authentic philosophical existence in the modern world. They will do so if they are willing to commit themselves to a purpose that St. Thomas himself never undertook to carry out, namely, to be philosophers in their own name and in the first person singular. The Thomism of the future, if there is to be a Thomistic philosophy, cannot be like the Thomism of the past, and particularly like the rationalist Thomism of the latter nineteenth century. If the original Thomism of the thirteenth century was not a philosophy, then there can be a philosophical Thomism in the future only if it loses its proper name and gains the personal engagement of living philosophers who are willing to guide themselves as philosophers by the principles and the spirit of the philosophy used by St. Thomas in his theology. If a man is a philosopher and a Thomist, then he is a disciple, not of the past, but of the present and the future; within his own world, his aim can be only to give a genuine philosophical life to the principles that St. Thomas used

in another day and under other conditions
of human culture.

To think of speaking of the future sug-
gests that, in some sense, the past has come
to an end. I hope indeed that the fragmen-
tation of St. Thomas has come to an end.
I hope that we shall undertake to build
our own Christian philosophy, not by detaching fragments from his theology, but
by risking our own intellectual lives in the
world of today. These lives will be informed by the personalist impetus of St.
Thomas' metaphysics but managed by our
own engagement and undertaken in our
own name. And if we create it, our own philosophy will be a genuine personalism, not
only engaged in everything human within
its own world, but also drawing the life of
man to that edge of existence where it can
be faithful to itself only by making its
knowledge and its love a dialogue with
God. Whether such a philosophy will exist
in the future remains to be seen. I am not
a prophet, and I have presented it in this
lecture as a lesson from the past. There
was a man in the thirteenth century who

created the intellectualism that is the permanent source of this ideal. Should it come into existence, it will be the philosophy of those who create it, and it will bear their names; but it is no less certain that the name of St. Thomas will be visible in the signatures of his intellectual children.

The Aquinas Lectures

Published by the Marquette University Press,
Milwaukee 3, Wisconsin

St. Thomas and the Life of Learning (1937) by
Fr. John F. McCormick, S.J., professor of
philosophy, Loyola University.

St. Thomas and the Gentiles (1938) by Morti-
mer J. Adler, Ph.D., director of the Institute
of Philosophical Research, San Francisco,
Calif.

St. Thomas and the Greeks (1939) by Anton C.
Pegis, Ph.D., professor of philosophy, Pontifical Institute of Mediaeval Studies, Toronto.

The Nature and Functions of Authority (1940)
by Yves Simon, Ph.D., professor of philosophy of social thought, University of Chicago.

St. Thomas and Analogy (1941) by Fr. Gerald
B. Phelan, Ph.D., professor of philosophy, St.
Michael's College, Toronto.

St. Thomas and the Problem of Evil (1942) by
Jacques Maritain, Ph.D., professor *emeritus*
of philosophy, Princeton University.

Humanism and Theology (1943) by Werner Jaeger, Ph.D., Litt.D., University professor, Harvard University.

The Nature and Origins of Scientism (1944) by John Wellmuth.

Cicero in the Courtroom of St. Thomas Aquinas (1945) by E. K. Rand, Ph.D., Litt.D., LL.D., Pope professor of Latin, *emeritus*, Harvard University.

St. Thomas and Epistemology (1946) by Fr. Louis-Marie Regis, O.P., Th.L., Ph.D., director of the Albert the Great Institute of Mediaeval Studies, University of Montreal.

St. Thomas and the Greek Moralists (1947, Spring) by Vernon J. Bourke, Ph.D., professor of philosophy, St. Louis University, St. Louis, Missouri.

History of Philosophy and Philosophical Education (1947, Fall) by Étienne Gilson of the *Académie française,* director of studies and professor of the history of Mediaeval philosophy, Pontifical Institute of Mediaeval Studies, Toronto.

The Natural Desire for God (1948) by Fr. William R. O'Connor, S.T.L., Ph.D., professor of dogmatic theology, St. Joseph's Seminary, Dunwoodie, N.Y.

St. Thomas and the World State (1949) by Robert M. Hutchins, Chancellor of the University of Chicago.

Method in Metaphysics (1950) by Fr. Robert J. Henle, S.J., dean of the graduate school, St. Louis University, St. Louis, Missouri.

Wisdom and Love in St. Thomas Aquinas (1951) by Étienne Gilson of the *Académie française,* director of studies and professor of the history of Mediaeval philosophy, Pontifical Institute of Mediaeval Studies, Toronto.

The Good in Existential Metaphysics (1952) by Elizabeth G. Salmon, associate professor of philosophy in the graduate school, Fordham University.

St. Thomas and the Object of Geometry (1953) by Vincent Edward Smith, Ph.D., professor of philosophy, University of Notre Dame.

Realism and Nominalism Revisited (1954) by Henry Veatch, Ph.D., professor of philosophy, Indiana University.

Imprudence in St. Thomas Aquinas (1955) by Charles J. O'Neil, Ph.D., professor of philosophy, Marquette University.

The Truth That Frees (1956) by Fr. Gerard Smith, S.J., Ph.D., professor and chairman of the department of philosophy, Marquette University.

St. Thomas and the Future of Metaphysics (1957) by Fr. Joseph Owens, C.Ss.R., associate professor of philosophy, Pontifical Institute of Mediaeval Studies, Toronto.

Thomas and the Physics of 1958: A Confrontation (1958) by Henry Margenau, Ph.D., Eugene Higgins professor of physics and natural philosophy, Yale University.

Metaphysics and Ideology (1959) by Wm. Oliver Martin, professor of philosophy, University of Rhode Island.

Language, Truth and Poetry (1960) by Victor M. Hamm, Ph.D., professor of English, Marquette University.

Metaphysics and Historicity (1961) by Emil L. Fackenheim, Ph.D., associate professor of philosophy, University of Toronto.

The Lure of Wisdom (1962) by James D. Collins, Ph.D., professor of philosophy, St. Louis University.

Religion and Art (1963) by Paul Weiss, Ph.D. Sterling Professor of philosophy, Yale University.

St. Thomas and Philosophy (1964) by Anton C. Pegis, of the Pontifical Institute of Mediaeval Studies, University of Toronto.

Uniform format, cover and binding.